HEINEMANN GUIDED READERS
**ELEMENTARY LEVEL**

EVELYN DAVIES AND PETER TOWN

# The Man With No Name

D1324266

HEINEMANN

**ELEMENTARY LEVEL**

*Series Editor*: John Milne

The Heinemann Guided Readers provide a choice of enjoyable reading material for learners of English. The series is published at five levels – Starter, Beginner, Elementary, Intermediate and Upper. At **Elementary Level**, the control of content and language has the following main features:

**Information Control**

Stories have straightforward plots and a restricted number of main characters. Information which is vital to the understanding of the story is clearly presented and repeated when necessary. Difficult allusion and metaphor are avoided and cultural backgrounds are made explicit.

**Structure Control**

Students will meet those grammatical features which they have already been taught in their elementary course of studies. Other grammatical features occasionally occur with which the students may not be so familiar, but their use is made clear through context and reinforcement. This ensures that the reading as well as being enjoyable provides a continual learning situation for the students. Sentences are kept short – a maximum of two clauses in nearly all cases – and within sentences there is a balanced use of simple adverbial and adjectival phrases. Great care is taken with pronoun reference.

**Vocabulary Control**

At **Elementary Level** there is a limited use of a carefully controlled vocabulary of approximately 1,100 basic words. At the same time, students are given some opportunity to meet new or unfamiliar words in contexts where their meaning is obvious. The meaning of words introduced in this way is reinforced by repetition. Help is also given to the students in the form of vivid illustrations which are closely related to the text.

# Contents

At the end of each chapter, you will see this symbol. When you see this symbol, look at the questions in *Points for Understanding* on pages 53–59.

# The Man With No Name

# 1

# 0300 Hours: The Warning

It was a dark night. There was no moon. It was a still night. There was no wind. But Mary Wallace was awake. Why?

Mary got up and looked out of her bedroom window. She did not see anything. She did not hear anything. There was no light and no sound.

The nearest village was four miles away. There was no telephone in Mary's cottage and no houses nearby. Mary Wallace lived alone.

Suddenly, the sky lit up for a second. For a second, there was light. Then, quickly, the sky was dark again. There was no light, and no sound.

Mary shivered. She had seen something, but what was it? Lightning? Perhaps. She did not know. Mary felt cold. She went back to bed and fell asleep.

COMPREHENSION BREAK

*Mary got up and looked out of her bedroom window.*

## 2

# 0800 Hours: The Plane

Next morning, Mary left the cottage. She was going shopping in the village four miles away. She carried a rucksack on her shoulder. The rucksack was light, and Mary walked quickly.

Mary started to climb up the hill behind her cottage. On top of the hill, there was a wood. Through the wood, on the other side of the hill, there was a valley. In the valley there was a small airfield.

Thirty years ago, the airfield had closed and now grass grew on the runway. Every week, Mary walked over the old runway. It was the quickest way to the village and the shops.

It was a bright, clear morning and Mary felt happy. The sun was shining on the grass, and the air was clean and fresh. Mary loved the bright, clear air in the north of Scotland. She liked living alone in Scotland. It was so quiet, so peaceful, so easy to write her books here.

Soon Mary reached the wood on the top of the hill. It was darker in the wood, still and silent. But soon Mary left the wood, and the sun shone again. At the top of the hill, Mary stopped for a moment and took a deep breath. She was ready to climb down into the valley.

First she looked up at the clear blue sky. Then she started to climb down the hill. Then Mary looked down at the old runway. And suddenly, for a second, her breath stopped.

*Mary started to climb up the hill behind her cottage.*

Mary had a shock. She closed her eyes for a second. Then she opened them again. There was a jet aircraft on the old runway.

The huge jet filled the small airfield. The sun shone on the plane's wings. The long grass covered the plane's wheels. And everything was silent and still.

Mary stopped and stood still. Then she thought quickly. It must be an accident. The plane had crashed. She must get help. She must look for people, and get help for the passengers.

She started to run quickly down the hill. Then she suddenly stopped and stood still again. Something was wrong. She looked down at the plane again. Everything was silent. She saw no one and she heard nothing. There was no sound and nothing moved. Were all the people in the plane dead?

Mary walked slowly now, down the hill. As she walked, she looked at the aircraft. She saw no damage. Nothing was scratched or broken. But there was no one, no sound, nothing.

At the bottom of the hill, Mary stopped again. She heard something now. It was the sound of music. Mary saw something too. The passenger ramp was down. The steps led from the open door into the long grass. The sound of music came from the open cabin door.

Mary shouted. No one answered. She ran quickly over the grass to the aircraft. At the bottom of the ramp, she stopped again and shouted very loudly. Again, no one answered. But the sound of music still came from the open cabin door.

Mary dropped her rucksack and ran up the ramp and into the plane.

The plane was empty – there was no one in it. Mary walked quickly, along the gangway, to the front of the plane. She found no one. No one alive or dead. She walked back slowly and looked at all the passenger seats. The seats were empty. There was no one alive or dead on the plane. Where were the passengers?

Mary dropped her rucksack and ran up the ramp and into the plane.

Mary walked back again to the front of the plane. She looked again at the empty seats. Where were the crew? At the front of the plane, Mary put her hand on the crew door. Then, for the second time that morning, her breath stopped. A hand tapped her shoulder, and a voice said, 'Is this yours?'

It was a man. He was carrying Mary's rucksack.

'My name is Ned Harding,' he said. 'I was walking to the village when I saw the plane . . .'

'There's no one here,' said Mary. 'There's nobody on the plane.'

Mary and Ned searched the plane together. Together they called, but no one answered. Together they shouted, but no one answered. There were no passengers and no crew.

Ned found food and drink in the galley. Mary found a warm cup of coffee in front of one of the seats. But they did not find the passenger list, and they did not find any hand luggage.

There was no damage. Nothing was broken. Everything was tidy.

'This plane did not crash,' said Ned. 'It *landed.*'

'Yes,' said Mary, 'but where are the passengers and the crew?'

Mary opened her rucksack and took out a notebook. She sat down near the galley, at the front of the plane. She began to make some notes.

Mary stopped writing and looked at Ned. He was searching the passenger seats. Suddenly he bent down and picked up a piece of paper. He looked at it quickly and put it in his pocket. Mary watched him. She got up and followed Ned down the plane.

Ned was bending over a seat. When he stood up, he had something in his hand. Then he saw Mary behind him.

Ned had a luggage label in his hand. He gave it to Mary.

'Have a look,' he said. Then he walked off again down the plane.

'Wait,' said Mary quietly. 'What have you got in your pocket?' Ned stopped, and was silent for a second. Then he put his hand in his pocket and walked back to Mary.

'It's a landing card,' he said. He gave it to Mary. Mary read the names on the card.

'Who are Mrs Charles Abbs and Sarah Abbs?'

'They are the pilot's wife and child,' said Ned quietly. 'They had a lot of luggage with them.'

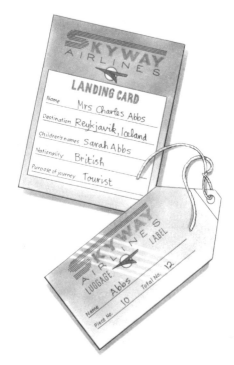

Mary said, 'How do y. . .' Then she stopped.

'Let's sit down,' Mary said. 'I want to think about the facts.'

Mary and Ned sat in the back of the plane. Mary showed Ned the list of facts in her notebook. Together they looked at the facts, but they did not understand them. Ned closed his eyes. He was thinking.

Mary wrote some questions in her notebook but she did not show the questions to Ned Harding. Then Ned opened his eyes.

'Come on,' he said suddenly, 'let's go to the flight deck.'

Ned ran quickly down the gangway towards the front of the plane. He went through the galley and onto the flight deck. Mary tore the page from her notebook and followed Ned.

When did plane l
How did plane
Where did passe
Where did Ned c
Why did Ned
How did Ned know

**2**

COMPREHENSION
BREAK

# 3

# 0900 Hours: The Flight Deck

The flight deck was empty. For a moment, Mary and Ned stood silently together. They looked at the control panel, but it did not tell them anything. Suddenly Ned said, 'What time is it?'

Mary looked at her watch. 'It's nine o'clock,' she said. 'Why?'

'Look at the flight deck clock,' answered Ned. Mary looked at the control panel again. The clock said 7 o'clock.

'What does that tell us?' she asked.

'Nothing,' answered Ned. 'We need the flight plan.'

'There's something under the pilot's seat,' said Mary. Ned bent down and picked up a map.

'Good,' he said, 'now we can learn something.' He sat in the pilot's seat, opened the flight plan, and looked at it carefully.

Mary looked over Ned's shoulder.

'What does it tell us?' she asked.

'Well,' said Ned, 'it tells us the flight number, and it tells us the route. But it tells us something else. Look at the flight plan carefully, and then look again at the control panel.'

Mary shook her head. She did not understand.

'Look at the flight plan,' said Ned. 'What does it tell you?'

'Well,' said Mary, 'this was flight 247. It was flying from the Lebanon to New York. It was due in Reykjavik to refuel at 0700 hours today.'

'Yes,' said Ned. 'Now the control panel clock stopped at 0700 hours which is . . .?'

18

*The flight deck clock said 7 o'clock.*

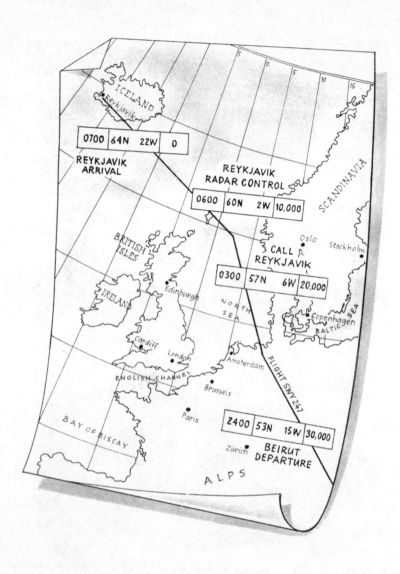

ICELAND
Reykjavik

| 0700 | 64N | 22W | 0 |

REYKJAVIK
ARRIVAL

REYKJAVIK
RADAR CONTROL

| 0600 | 60N | 2W | 10,000 |

SCANDINAVIA

BRITISH
ISLES

CALL
REYKJAVIK

Oslo    Stockholm

| 0300 | 57N | 6W | 20,000 |

IRELAND    Edinburgh

NORTH
SEA

Copenhagen    SEA
BALTIC

Cardiff
London
Amsterdam

ENGLISH CHANNEL

Brussels

FLIGHT SWY 247

Paris

BAY OF BISCAY

| 2400 | 53N | 15W | 30,000 |

Zürich    BEIRUT
DEPARTURE

A L P S

'Look at the flight plan carefully, and then look again at
the control panel.'

'Reykjavik arrival time,' said Mary.

'What is the compass bearing for Reykjavik?' asked Ned.

Mary looked at the map. 'Sixty-four degrees north and twenty-two west,' she answered.

'Yes,' said Ned quietly, 'and now look at the control panel.' Mary did. The instruments on the panel read 64°N and 22°W, and the clock had stopped at 7 o'clock.

Mary was clever. She understood quickly.

'But it's impossible,' Mary whispered, 'the panel is wrong. The instruments say the plane is in Reykjavik. But it isn't. The plane is not *there*, it's *here*, in Scotland.'

'Yes,' said Ned, 'here in the middle of Scotland, on an old airfield, with no passengers and no crew.'

Mary and Ned left the flight deck. They went through the galley, into the passenger cabin. They sat down in two passenger seats and looked at the map again. Mary got her pencil and drew a line from the flight path to Scotland.

'Look,' she said, 'the plane left the flight path just before 3 o'clock last night. Last night I woke up about 3 o'clock. I don't know why. Something woke me. I got up and went to the window. And just after 3 o'clock I saw a light. Perhaps the plane crashed then.'

'It didn't *crash*,' said Ned quietly. 'It *landed*.'

'Oh yes,' said Mary thoughtfully, 'Perhaps the light I saw was a signal.'

'A signal?' said Ned. 'You mean somebody here in Scotland made a landing light, and helped the plane to land?'

'Yes,' said Mary. 'Remember, the plane's instruments were wrong. The instruments all say the plane is in Reykjavik. Perhaps the pilot thought he *was* in Reykjavik. He saw signal lights and landed here.'

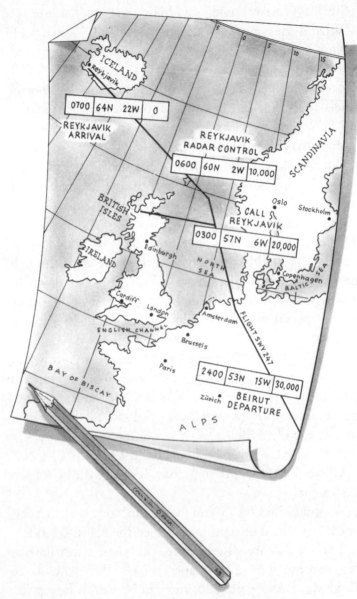

Mary got her pencil and drew a line from the flight path
to Scotland.

'No,' said Ned, 'you don't know anything about flying. It didn't happen like that.'

'But what was the light?' asked Mary. 'What happened at 3 o'clock?'

'I don't know,' said Ned thoughtfully, 'I don't know.' He folded the flight plan carefully and put it in his pocket.

**3**

COMPREHENSION BREAK

# 4

# 1000 Hours: The Man

Suddenly, the music stopped.

'The tape's finished,' said Ned.

The plane was silent now. And then they heard a sound. They heard a tapping noise. Mary and Ned stood up slowly together. They listened, but the plane was silent again. And then the noise came again. A scratching noise, like an animal.

Mary and Ned shouted. No one answered but the scratching, tapping noise continued. It came from the back of the plane.

Mary and Ned ran to the back of the plane, and then stood still. Silence. And then they heard it again. A gentle tapping noise, louder now. The noise came from inside the lavatory door.

'We forgot to look in the lavatory!' cried Mary.

Ned grabbed the handle, but the door was locked on the inside. Mary put her face close to the door.

'Is somebody in there?' she called gently. Silence. They knocked. They called. They shouted. No one answered. But there was still a tapping from inside, quieter now.

'Break the lock!' shouted Mary.

Ned threw himself at the door, but it did not move. Mary and Ned together threw themselves at the door. Again it did not move. Then they threw themselves at the door a third time, with all their strength.

The wood cracked. But the lock did not break. The noise stopped.

'Stand back,' said Ned. He kicked the lock hard. The wood cracked again, but the lock did not break. Ned kicked at the lock harder, with all his strength, and this time the lock broke.

The door swung inwards. It was dark inside. At first, they did not see anything. Then they saw a dark shape on the floor. It was a man.

The man opened his mouth, but no sound came.

'What happened?' asked Mary.

The man did not turn his head. He did not look at Mary. He looked at Ned.

'He can't hear,' said Mary. 'He's deaf.'

The man opened his mouth and tried to speak, but he made no sound.

Ned said, 'He can't speak. He's dumb.'

The man could not hear or speak. He was deaf and dumb.

Ned and Mary lifted the man and took him to a seat. Mary got her notebook and pencil. The man could not hear, he could not speak, but he could write!

Mary wrote:

What happened?

What is your name?

Where are the passengers?

Mary put the notebook and pencil into the man's hands. The man wrote quickly.

Mary and Ned looked at the notebook. Then Mary and Ned looked at the man. They looked at the paper, at the man, and at each other. It was not English . . . they did not understand it.

Mary spoke to the man again, very slowly. The man shook his head. He looked frightened. Mary and Ned looked at each other again. The man could not hear their questions. They could not speak to the man. They did not understand what the man wrote.

Mary and Ned did not understand any of the clues in the plane.

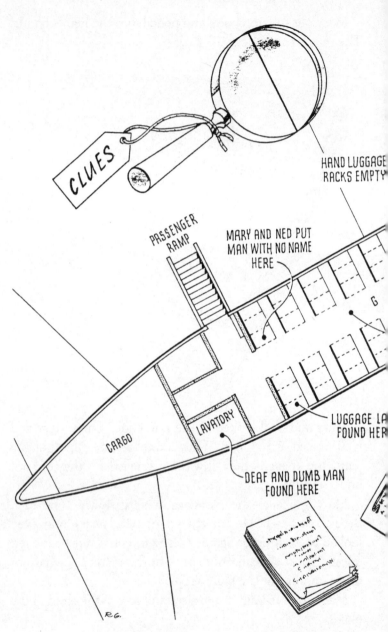

CLUES

HAND LUGGAGE
RACKS EMPTY

PASSENGER
RAMP

MARY AND NED PUT
MAN WITH NO NAME
HERE

G

LUGGAGE LA
FOUND HER

LAVATORY

CARGO

DEAF AND DUMB MAN
FOUND HERE

R.G.

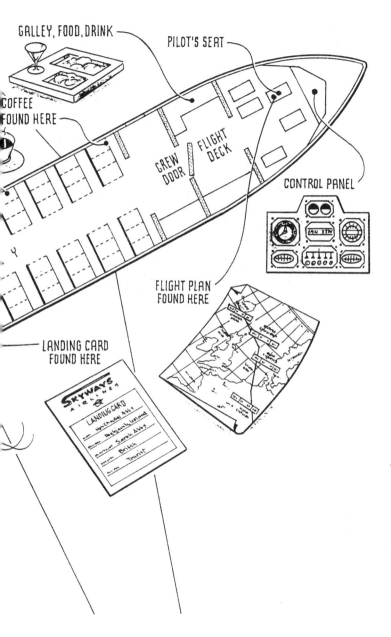

GALLEY, FOOD, DRINK

PILOT'S SEAT

COFFEE
FOUND HERE

CREW
DOOR

FLIGHT
DECK

CONTROL PANEL

FLIGHT PLAN
FOUND HERE

LANDING CARD
FOUND HERE

SKYWAYS
AIRLINES
LANDING CARD

Mary and Ned called him the "Man With No Name". Together, they looked at the Man's writing, but it told them nothing.

The Man With No Name fell asleep. Mary went to the galley to look for a blanket for the Man With No Name. Ned sat next to the Man and looked at the notes in Mary's notebook. The plane was silent again.

Mary found a blanket in the galley and came back quietly down the gangway. Then she stopped. She saw Ned bending over the Man With No Name. Ned had a piece of paper in his left hand, and his right hand was in the Man's pocket. Mary was behind Ned now. She tapped him sharply on the shoulder.

'What are you doing?' she said angrily.

'I want to know who he is,' said Ned. 'I'm looking for some identification. Help me to look in his pockets.'

'No,' said Mary firmly, 'the Man is asleep!'

'It will only take a moment,' said Ned quickly. 'We must find out his name.'

'Why?' said Mary. 'That is not our job. We are not the police. We must find help now. We must tell the police.'

Mary looked at the Man. He was still asleep. She put the blanket over him.

'We must take this man to a doctor,' she said.

'Yes, of course,' said Ned quickly, 'but it will only take a moment to find out his name.'

Ned held out the piece of paper in his hand. It was torn from Mary's notebook, and Ned had written some headings on it. Mary was worried, but she was interested. Slowly she took the paper out of Ned's hand.

'Please,' said Ned, 'please help. It will only take a moment.'

*Ned had a piece of paper in his left hand, and his right hand was in the Man's pocket.*

*Mary looked at the Man. He was still asleep. She put the blanket over him.*

Mary looked at the piece of paper, and Ned turned to the Man.

'There is nothing in his pockets,' said Ned. 'No identification. No passport. No papers. No letters. Not even a ticket.'

On the paper, next to 'Name and Address', Mary wrote UNKNOWN. Then she looked at the next heading.

'How old is he?' she asked. Ned looked at the sleeping man.

'Oh – middle aged,' he replied, '40 or 50.'

Mary wrote this fact on the paper next to 'Age', and then looked at the next heading.

'Where does he come from?' she asked.

Ned picked up Mary's notebook and looked at the writing of the Man With No Name.

'What language is it?' asked Ned. 'Polish? Spanish? Arabic?'

'I don't know,' Mary answered, 'but it certainly isn't English.'

Mary wrote UNKNOWN again on the piece of paper.

'Wait a minute,' said Ned. 'I want to look at his clothes.' Ned took the man's coat and looked for a shop label.

'That's unusual,' said Ned. 'There are no labels on his clothes.'

Mary looked again at Ned's notes.

'What's his job?' she asked.

Ned looked again at the Man's clothes. The clothes were clean, but not new. They were tidy, but not smart. Then Ned looked at the Man's hands. They were clean, smooth and soft, and the nails were quite long.

'I don't know,' said Ned. 'I don't know. I don't think he works with his hands.'

Name

Address

Age

Nationality

Occupation

Appearance

Mary wrote something on the paper.

'Is there anything unusual about his appearance?' Mary asked.

Ned looked at the sleeping man carefully.

'He's got red hair,' said Ned, 'and a small scar on his left hand.'

Mary wrote this down on the paper.

'Anything else?' she asked.

'Nothing,' said Ned. 'No labels on his clothes, nothing in his pockets, no money, no papers, nothing. He is a very mysterious, unknown man.'

Mary finished writing her notes and stood up. 'We must get help now,' she said firmly.

4

COMPREHENSION BREAK

# 1100 Hours: The Investigator

The Man With No Name was still asleep.

'Who is he?' said Ned thoughtfully.

'And who are you?' answered Mary. 'How did you get here?'

'I told you,' said Ned. 'My name is Ned Harding, and I was walking to the village when I saw the plane . . .'

'You know too much,' said Mary. 'Who are you? And how did you know the pilot's name?'

For a moment, Ned did not answer. Then he said quietly, 'And who are *you*? What are you doing here? Have you got any identification?'

Mary was angry. 'I live here,' she said. 'My name is Mary Wallace, and I can prove it. I can show you my driving licence. Now, once again, who are you?'

'All right,' said Ned. 'My name is Ned Harding. I'm an investigator. I'm an insurance investigator. I'm an airline insurance investigator. I can prove it too. Here's my card.'

'All right,' said Mary, 'but what are you doing here, in Scotland?'

'It's a long story, Mary,' replied Ned. 'This isn't the first plane to disappear. Planes disappear. Boats disappear. People disappear. Sometimes the planes are found. Like this one. There's food and drink. But there are no people. Sometimes the boats are found. There are cigarettes, newspapers, food, but no people. It's like the old Marie Celeste.'

'Marie Celeste?' asked Mary.

'A ship,' replied Ned. 'It disappeared about a hundred years ago. It left New York with a full crew. But later it was found at sea. It was empty. There was no damage, but there was no crew. And they never found the crew, alive or dead.'

'You are right,' said Mary. 'This plane is just like the Marie Celeste.'

INVESTIGATOR

Mr. T.P.N. Harding

IS AUTHORISED TO INVESTIGATE
INSURANCE CLAIMS ON BEHALF OF

SKYWAY AIRLINES

DRIVING LICENCE

NAME Ms Mary Wallace
ADDRESS The Auld Manor
Flawes, Scotland

VEHICLE NO. PYP 579 G

'But why don't the newspapers say anything?' asked Mary.

'They do say something,' answered Ned. He put his hand in his pocket and took out some press cuttings.

'Look at these, Mary,' he said.

'They all disappeared here, in the North of Scotland,' said Mary.

'Yes,' said Ned. 'I'm here to investigate for an insurance company.' Ned put his hand in his pocket and took out a map.

'Look at this, Mary,' he said, 'read this map.'

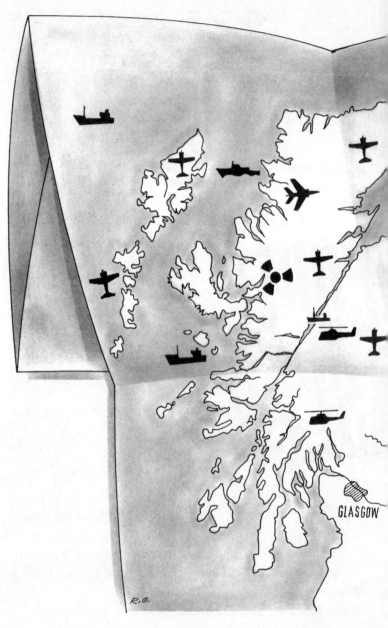

GLASGOW

R.G.

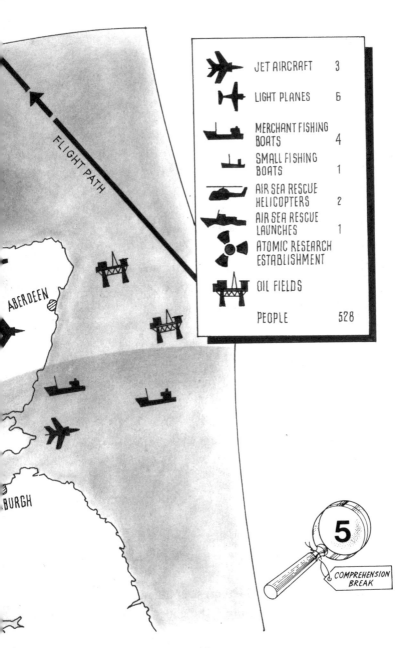

FLIGHT PATH

| | JET AIRCRAFT | 3 |
| | LIGHT PLANES | 6 |
| | MERCHANT FISHING BOATS | 4 |
| | SMALL FISHING BOATS | 1 |
| | AIR SEA RESCUE HELICOPTERS | 2 |
| | AIR SEA RESCUE LAUNCHES | 1 |
| | ATOMIC RESEARCH ESTABLISHMENT | |
| | OIL FIELDS | |
| | PEOPLE | 528 |

ABERDEEN

BURGH

5

COMPREHENSION BREAK

41

# 6

# 1200 Hours: The Messages

Mary looked at the map carefully. Then she turned to Ned.

'All these planes, boats and people have disappeared,' she said, 'and nobody asks questions. Why don't the police do something? Why doesn't the Government do something?'

'I don't know, Mary,' said Ned. 'That's why I'm here. I must find out why people leave the planes and boats. Where do they go? What happens to all these people? We never see them again, and no one asks questions.'

'Well, I'm going to ask a lot of questions about *this* plane,' said Mary. 'Why did it land here? How did it land? Why did the passengers leave? Where did they go? Who is the Man With No Name?'

'You are right, Mary,' said Ned. 'This time it's different. This time we have found the plane. We must find some answers.'

'Yes,' said Mary, 'but we have searched the plane and found nothing. And the Man With No Name can't speak. We must go to the police now and report it, and we must take the Man to a doctor.'

'Wait, Mary,' said Ned. 'There must be some clue in the plane. Let me think.'

Suddenly, Ned stood up. 'Come on, Mary,' he said. 'Let's look again. There's something else on the flight deck.'

Mary and Ned left the man sleeping in his seat. They ran along the gangway, through the galley, and onto the flight deck.

QUESTIONS

| ! | ? |
|---|---|
| Instruments wrong. Light seen at 0300 hrs. | Why did it land? When did it land? |
| Plane undamaged. Family on plane with a lot of luggage. | How did he land? Did the Pilot know something? |
| Has no identification. Does not write in English. | Who is he? Is he foreign? |
| 528 People have disappeared. All in Scotland. | Why don't the Police do something? Does the Government know something? |
| There is no hand luggage, warm coffee, music playing. | Where did they go? Why did they leave the plane? Did the passeng |

On the flight deck, Ned searched the instruments.

'What are you looking for?' asked Mary.

'The flight voice recorder,' answered Ned. 'Here it is.'

Ned sat in the pilot's seat, and Mary sat on his right in the co-pilot's seat. Ned found the switch, and turned on the voice recorder.

Mary and Ned sat and listened to the tape. When it stopped, they were silent for a moment. Then they played the message again and Mary wrote the message in her notebook.

'What does that tell us?' asked Mary.

'Nothing,' said Ned. He put his head in his hands. Mary put her hand on Ned's shoulder.

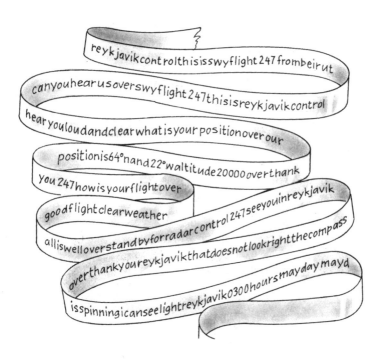

reykjavikcontrolthisisswyflight247frombeirut

canyouhearusoverswyflight247thisisreykjavikcontrol

hearyouloudandclearwhatisyourpositionoverour

positionis64°nand22°waltitude20000overthank

you247howisyourflightover

goodflightclearweather

alliswelloverstandbyforradarcontrol247seeyouinreykjavik

overthankyoureykjavikthatdoesnotlookrightthecompass

isspinningicanseelightreykjavik0300hoursmaydaymayd

'Don't worry,' she said, 'we still have one clue. There is still the Man With No Name.'

'You are right, Mary,' said Ned. 'He is the only clue. Give me your notebook, Mary.'

Ned took the notebook and turned back the pages. Together they looked again at the Man's writing.

'I don't understand it,' said Ned. '*.deppots enalp ehT*. It certainly isn't English.'

'Wait,' said Mary, grabbing the notebook.

'Look, Ned. The capital letters are on the right, and the question marks are on the left.' Mary was very excited.

'Ned,' she said, 'read the first word on the right backwards.'

'T..h..e – the,' said Ned slowly.

deppots enalp ehT
.tuohs ton dluoc I
ton dluow rood ehT
.nepo
eht era erehW
?sregnessap
?efiw ym si erehW

'Read it all backwards, Ned,' said Mary excitedly. 'Write it all down from right to left.'

Ned did. The Man With No Name *did* write English. But he did not write from left to right; he wrote from right to left.

Mary said, 'It's very strange. Perhaps he had a shock. A big shock. Perhaps the shock made him deaf and dumb, and perhaps it made him write backwards.'

'Perhaps,' said Ned. 'But now we can understand him. Now we can ask him questions.'

'Yes,' said Mary. 'But first we must take him to a doctor. Then we can ask him questions.'

'No,' said Ned. 'I must do something now. This time I was here first. This time we've got the plane. We've got this message from the voice recorder, and we've got the Man With No Name. He must know something. We can read his writing now. First the questions, then the doctor, then the police.'

Mary stood up and picked up her notebook. She smiled.

'Come on, Ned,' she said. 'Let's ask the Man some questions and then take him to a doctor.'

Mary left the flight deck and Ned followed her quickly. Mary ran down the gangway, and then stopped suddenly.

At the back of the plane, Mary's breath stopped for the third time that morning. The Man's seat was empty.

'Ned,' whispered Mary, 'he's not here.'

There were no passengers on Flight SWY 247 Beirut to Reykjavik.

COMPREHENSION BREAK

'Ned,' whispered Mary, 'he's not here.'

## Note for the Student

This is a mystery story. There is no explanation. But there are many facts and clues. Some are in words, some are in the pictures. These can be used to make *theories* like the ones on page 50.

Look again at the questions in the *Points for Understanding* section on pages 53–59.

Then, use your answers and your own ideas to explain the facts and finish the story.

## Note for the Teacher: Further Reading

This is a fictitious story loosely based on things which happened in an area called The Bermuda Triangle.

If students are interested in this kind of story, they can read more about it in the books below which have been translated into several languages.

*The Bermuda Triangle*   C Berlitz
*Limbo of the Lost*   J Spencer
*The Great Lakes Triangle*   J Gourley

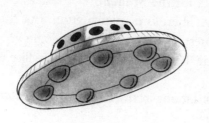

compass

spinning

deppots enalp ehT

WAR
DEPARTMENT

DEAF MUTE
FOUND IN
EMPTY BOAT

14 days in an open boat
without any form of id-
entification, juton...
...ular man...

I saw
a light!

## Disappeara
## of Politiciar

Eighteen days after
returning from hol-
iday...
Peter...

Why don't the
police and
government do
something?

No...
asks...

R.6,

51

# POINTS
# FOR
# UNDERSTANDING

# Points for Understanding

## 1

### To Answer

1 What did Mary see at 3 am?
2 What did she think it was?
3 What else do you think it could have been?

## 2

### To Answer

1 Why did Mary like living alone in Scotland?
2 What kind of airfield did the plane land on?
3 What did Mary and Ned find on the plane?
4 How much luggage did the pilot's family have?
5 Why were they travelling on the plane?

### To Do

6 Look at Mary's notes on page 16. She wrote them in a hurry. Write them out in full.
7 What questions did Mary want to ask? Complete her questions at the bottom of page 17.

When did plane l
How did plane
Where did passe
Where did Ned c
Why did Ned
How did Ned know

0300 Hours
Something woke me
Saw light
Did not hear anything

0815 Hours
Found empty plane
Music playing
Plane landed, did not crash

0830 Hours
Ned came
Searched plane together

FOUND ✓          DID NOT FIND ✗

FACTS

### To Answer

1 What did Mary and Ned find on the flight deck?
2 Where did they find it?
3 What time was the plane due in Reykjavik?
4 What was wrong with the plane's instruments?
5 When did the plane leave its flight path?
6 What did Mary say about the pilot?
7 Mary said, 'Perhaps . . . he saw signal lights and landed here.' Who is *he* and where is *here*?
8 Did Ned agree with Mary?

### To Do

9 Add some new facts to your list from Chapter 2.
10 Decide what you would do next, if you were Mary or Ned.

## 4

*To Answer*

1  When did Mary and Ned hear a noise on the plane?
2  Where did the noise come from?
3  How did Mary and Ned open the door?
4  Why did Mary ask the Man to write his message?
5  Where did Ned put the Man? (Use the drawing on pages 28 and 29 and give a full answer.)
6  Why did Ned look in the Man's pockets?
7  What was unusual about the Man's clothes?
8  Why did Ned say, 'I don't think he works with his hands.'?

*To Do*

9  Make a list of everything you know about the Man With No Name. Add the new facts to your notes.
10  Look at Ned's notes on page 34 and complete them.

Name
Address
Age
Nationality
Occupation
Appearance

# 5

## To Answer

1 What was Ned's job, and how did he prove it?
2 Why was Ned in Scotland?
3 How many of the newspaper headlines report clear weather?
4 What Government property was in that area of Scotland?
5 How many aircraft had disappeared in the area?
6 How many ships and boats had disappeared in the area?
7 How many people had disappeared in the area?
8 Why is the number of people bigger than the number of planes and boats?

## To Do

9 Study the newspaper headlines on pages 38 and 39 carefully. They all tell similar stories. What kind of stories are they?
10 Write a newspaper headline for the events in this book.

# 6

## To Answer

1 What was Ned looking for on the flight deck?
2 What two things did the pilot report at 0300 hours?
3 What was strange about the way the Man With No Name wrote English?
4 What did Mary think was the reason for this?
5 Was the Man With No Name travelling alone?
6 What did Mary want to do first?
7 What did Ned want to do first?
8 Look at Mary's questions on page 43. What do you think the last question should be?

## To Do

9 Write the message on page 46 so that it can be read from left to right.
10 Write out the tape message on page 45. It is a *conversation* between the pilot and Reykjavik airport. Put in all the punctuation. When you see the word OVER, leave it out, but start a new line.

**ELEMENTARY LEVEL**

Road to Nowhere *by John Milne*
The Black Cat *by John Milne*
Don't Tell Me What To Do *by Michael Hardcastle*
The Runaways *by Victor Canning*
The Red Pony *by John Steinbeck*
The Goalkeeper's Revenge and Other Stories *by Bill Naughton*
The Stranger *by Norman Whitney*
The Promise *by R.L. Scott-Buccleuch*
The Man With No Name *by Evelyn Davies and Peter Town*
The Cleverest Person in the World *by Norman Whitney*
Claws *by John Landon*
Z for Zachariah *by Robert C. O'Brien*
Tales of Horror *by Bram Stoker*
Frankenstein *by Mary Shelley*
Silver Blaze and Other Stories *by Sir Arthur Conan Doyle*
Tales of Ten Worlds *by Arthur C. Clarke*
The Boy Who Was Afraid *by Armstrong Sperry*
Room 13 and Other Ghost Stories *by M.R. James*
The Narrow Path *by Francis Selormey*
The Woman in Black *by Susan Hill*

For further information on the full selection of
Readers at all five levels in the series, please refer
to the Heinemann Guided Readers catalogue.

Heinemann English Language Teaching
A division of Heinemann Publishers (Oxford) Ltd
Halley Court, Jordan Hill, Oxford OX2 8EJ

OXFORD MADRID ATHENS PARIS FLORENCE PRAGUE
SÃO PAULO CHICAGO MELBOURNE AUCKLAND
SINGAPORE TOKYO GABORONE
JOHANNESBURG PORTSMOUTH (NH) IBADAN

ISBN 0 435 27201 2

Illustrated by Jerry Hoare and Richard Geiger
Typography by Adrian Hodgkins
Cover by Jamel Akib (Sharp Practice) and Threefold Design
Typeset in 11.5/14.5 pt Goudy
by Joshua Associates Ltd, Oxford
Printed and bound in Malta by Interprint Limited